6ª

# Lappish cooking

FROM FIRE AND FELL

**Photographs**
Jaakko Alatalo
Jorma Aula
Levin Matkailu

**Publisher**
Polarlehdet Oy

**Printed by**
Painolinna Oy, Savonlinna 1999

**Paper**
LumiArt Silk 150 g, Stora Enso Fine Paper, Oulu

**Translation**
Ulrike Knak, Elsa Sippel

ISBN 952-9762-18-6

# Päivikki Palosaari
# LAPPISH COOKING

## FROM FIRE AND FELL

# CONTENTS

**The art of living and eating**    7

**JANUARY**    9
Blood bread . . . . . . . . . . . . . . . . . . . . . 10
Grease porridge . . . . . . . . . . . . . . . . . 10
Lappish cheese . . . . . . . . . . . . . . . . . 10
Thoroughly salted meat à la Hullu Poro . . . . 10
Reindeer's liver and boletus sausages . . . . . 11
Tongue and liver with marinated
mustard sauce . . . . . . . . . . . . . . . . 11
Cloudberry fool . . . . . . . . . . . . . . . . 11
Reindeer blood sausages . . . . . . . . . . . . 12
Melted butter-onion sauce . . . . . . . . . . . 12
Carrot-lingonberry compote . . . . . . . . . . 12
'Kampsut' (blood patties) . . . . . . . . . . . 12

**FEBRUARY**    15
Garden angelica soup . . . . . . . . . . . . . . 16
Butter porridge . . . . . . . . . . . . . . . . . 16
Lingonberry soup . . . . . . . . . . . . . . . . 16
Oatmeal bread . . . . . . . . . . . . . . . . . . 16
Stuffed breast of willow grouse . . . . . . . . 17
Snow eggs . . . . . . . . . . . . . . . . . . . . 18
'Luikut' (marrow) . . . . . . . . . . . . . . . . 18

Reindeer back broth . . . . . . . . . . . . . . . 18
Meringue willow grouse . . . . . . . . . . . . . 18

**MARCH**    21
Potato porridge . . . . . . . . . . . . . . . . . 22
Barley flour bread . . . . . . . . . . . . . . . . 22
Sour milk bread . . . . . . . . . . . . . . . . . 22
Burbot roe and liver with butter . . . . . . . . 22
Escalope à la Hullu Poro . . . . . . . . . . . . 22
Love gruel . . . . . . . . . . . . . . . . . . . . 24
Dried meat . . . . . . . . . . . . . . . . . . . . 24
Dry meat broth . . . . . . . . . . . . . . . . . . 24
Raw whitefish with blueberry seasoning . . . . 24
Lingonberry snow on rye delicacy . . . . . . . 24
Lappish hut roast . . . . . . . . . . . . . . . . 25

**APRIL**    27
Sour wheat bread . . . . . . . . . . . . . . . . 28
Birch sap & cloudberry fool . . . . . . . . . . 28
Berry-rye flour porridge . . . . . . . . . . . . 28
Raw-spiced trout . . . . . . . . . . . . . . . . 28
Boletus stew . . . . . . . . . . . . . . . . . . . 28
Smoked trout . . . . . . . . . . . . . . . . . . 29

Thoroughly salted elk or reindeer roast
tai poronpaistia . . . . . . . . . . . . . . . . 29
Crowberry parfait . . . . . . . . . . . . . . . . 29

**MAY**    31
Slightly salted reindeer fillet . . . . . . . . . . 32
Tenoriver salmon with two sauces . . . . . . . 32
Brown bread . . . . . . . . . . . . . . . . . . . 32
Spring porridge . . . . . . . . . . . . . . . . . 34
Beet-barley grain-casserole . . . . . . . . . . . 34
Birch sap mead . . . . . . . . . . . . . . . . . . 34
Rhubarb-pie . . . . . . . . . . . . . . . . . . . 34
Marinated berries in honey cream . . . . . . . . 34

**JUNE**    37
Salmon in lingonberry sauce . . . . . . . . . . 38
Pretzel-shaped summer buns . . . . . . . . . . 38
Perch fillets with dandelion sauce . . . . . . . 38
Bread soup . . . . . . . . . . . . . . . . . . . . 40
Garden angelica juice . . . . . . . . . . . . . . 40
Nettle soup . . . . . . . . . . . . . . . . . . . . 40
Salmon soup . . . . . . . . . . . . . . . . . . . 40
Unripened cheese pudding . . . . . . . . . . . 40
Spruce shoots jam . . . . . . . . . . . . . . . . 41

## JULY     43

Rice porridge covered with drymeat ....... 44
Blackcurrant-leaf drink ............. 44
Garden angelica-pie ............. 44
Hors-d'œvre of the summer delicacies ...... 44
Rhubarb skim ................. 44
Salmon and reindeer with two sauces ...... 45
Morel sauce for reindeer ............. 45
Lingonberry sauce for the fish ........... 45
Cucumber-herb spread ............. 46
Cakes à la Taivaanvalkeat ........... 46

## AUGUST     49

A Lappish women's love-philtre .......... 50
Blueberry porridge ............... 50
'Puikula' potatoes in foil ............. 50
Boletus rolls ................. 50
Gelatinized reindeer tongue ............. 50
Blueberry-cloudberry fool ............. 51
Salmon-whitefish roll ............. 51
Potherbs sauce ............... 51
Spruce shoot butter ............. 52
Rowan berry wine ............. 52
Cloudberry pudding ............. 52

## SEPTEMBER     55

Katekeeta pudding ............. 56
Carrot-yeast bread ............. 56
Mushroom steaks ............. 56
Lingonberry fool ............... 56
Carrot timbale ............... 56
Smoked reindeer-mushroom soup ......... 57
Spruce shoot parfait ............. 57
Wood grouse roast ............. 57

## OCTOBER     59

Roast rabbit ................. 60
Rabbit terrine with currant sauce ......... 60
Fried pork gravy ............... 60
Salted vendace ............... 62
Mutton cabbage ............... 62
Turnip-wheat bread ............. 62
Whipped lingonberry pudding ......... 62
Currant sauce ............... 62
Vendace roe as hors-dœvre ......... 62
Mutton chops in garlic-herb-cream ......... 63
Lingonberry-cream pudding ......... 63
Carrot-oatchips ............... 63

## NOVEMBER     66

Buttermilk loaf ............... 67
Rye bread & raw-spiced salmon salad ..... 67
Mashed potato soup ............. 67
Carrot-lingonberry-compote ......... 67
Reindeer meat-cheese-pie ......... 68
Stuffed reindeer fillet ............. 68
Liqueur-pancakes fried on the
bottom of fireplace ............. 68

## DECEMBER     71

Cooked loaf ............... 72
Red raw-spiced salmon ............. 72
Lingonberry raw-spiced whitefish ......... 72
Reindeer calf aspic ............. 72
Reindeer roast ............... 72
Christmas-red Christmas fish ........... 73
Heavenly dish ............... 74
Sauteed reindeer ............. 74

## HULLU PORO'S COURAGEOUS LANDLADY     75

# THE ART OF LIVING AND EATING

The way of living in Lapland has always been of particular interest to me. No matter how difficult living conditions may have been, there had always been a way to get on. Own philosophies of life had to be developed and for thousands of years people in Lapland know that "water is the best cure for everything". Whatever ideas had arisen from these philosophies, in one or the other way they can be found again in the Lappish eating habits. Lapland's nature offers a bounty of delicacies, especially as the natural and pure ingredients guarantee an exquisite flavour. There are several reasons for the remarkable quality of Lappish food products, e.g. the nightless night of the Lappish summer. Due to low temperatures in winter bacteria cannot survive and no pesticides have to be put on the fields. Thus, a better taste can develop and food does not taste of fertilizer or the like.

The prerequisites couldn't be better and the time had come to integrate such a unique cuisine into modern gastronomy. And what else would you need except ideas, a strong interest in cooking and the desire to entertain visitors.

For me it was about time to write down some of the modern recipes of the 'Hullu Poro' restaurant. The booklet contains secrets of Lapland's cuisine good enough to please even the most demanding gourmet. By choosing ingredients only from Lapland's pure nature and by combinig ancient and traditional knowledge, a new art of eating could develop. Recipes in this book can also be found on Hullu Poro's menu. The book takes into account that each month has its own and typical range of ingredients. Thus, it introduces traditional as well as modern recipes, taking the natural availability of the ingredients into account. Even nowadays, food typical for the season, is on the daily menu in the village Sirkka in Kittilä. The Hullu Poro cuisine would also like to proceed with Tapio Sointu's Lappi à la carte - program.

*The Hullu Poro cookingteam - Riitta Jarva, Päivikki Palosaari, Tanja Sinervo and Mia Tarvainen.*

I hope you'll enjoy our kitchen - delicacies from fire and fell - !
*Päivikki Palosaari*

# JANUARY

First sunbeams can be seen on the fell's horizon. It's a pink and orange morning, the landscape is painted in pastel colours, the emerging light superseding 'kaamos'. There is a one hour gain in light every passing week. Step by step, slowly increasing.

The biting cold becomes visible when breathing out - white frost spreads in the air. It's the time for nutritious food. Still, as Christmas time has just passed people in Lapland have to live economically.

The oldest cow is slaughtered. Nourishing meals are prepared from the cow's blood and innards. After Christmas, people in Lapland enjoy thoroughly salted meat or the simple 'love gruel'. A special delicacy is Lappish cheese served with hot coffee.

The herb typical for January is juniper. Juniper berries can be picked at all times of the year. Nevertheless, they are best in autumn. Twigs can be taken throughout the year. Still, when preparing tea it's best to use fresh ones from the spring season - the time when they are rich in vitamins.

BLOOD BREAD . . . . . . . . . . . . . . . . . . . . 10

GREASE PORRIDGE . . . . . . . . . . . . . . . . 10

LAPPISH CHEESE . . . . . . . . . . . . . . . . . . 10

THOROUGHLY SALTED MEAT
À LA HULLU PORO . . . . . . . . . . . . . . . . . 10

REINDEER'S LIVER AND
BOLETUS SAUSAGES . . . . . . . . . . . . . . . . 11

TONGUE AND LIVER WITH
MARINATED MUSTARD SAUCE . . . . . . . . 11

CLOUDBERRY FOOL . . . . . . . . . . . . . . . . 11

REINDEER BLOOD SAUSAGES . . . . . . . . . . 12

MELTED BUTTER-ONION SAUCE . . . . . . . . 12

CARROT-LINGONBERRY COMPOTE . . . . . . 12

'KAMPSUT' (BLOOD PATTIES) . . . . . . . . . . 12

## BLOOD BREAD

| 1 1/2 litres blood |
| 1/2 litre water or homebrewed beer |
| 5 tablespoons yeast |
| 2 teaspoons salt |
| (2 teaspoons marjoram) |
| 1 1/2 kg barley flour |
| 1 1/2 kg rye flour |

Blend the yeast and spices in lukewarm water or beer and add to the blood mixture. Make bread with a hole in the middle of the rising dough and prick holes when the bread has risen. Bake in good oven temperature (225 centigrades). Keep the bread dry. Cut the blood bread e.g. into small pieces, dissolve them in cold water or milk and boil quickly. Serve with lingonberry jam.

## GREASE PORRIDGE

| spare ribs |
| 100 g butter or melted pork fat |
| 2 l water |
| 3 dl unground barley grains |
| salt |

Spread the grains on the bottom of an oven dish, and hot water and pork fat on top. Use enough pork fat to cover the surface completely. Let simmer in low heat for a couple of hours. Eat with sugar and milk.

## LAPPISH CHEESE

| 10 l milk |
| 2 tablespoons cheese rennet |
| 2 teaspoons salt |

Warm up the milk until handwarm. Stir in the rennet, mix and let the mixture curdle in a warm place. Mix the compound carefully and let it sink to the bottom of the saucepan. Pour the fluid away. Press the mixture with a skimmer to take away remaining fluid. Lift the cheese compound to the baking board with the help of a dense strainer to drain, then add salt. Place the dish on a baking sheet, as the fluid may drip to the bottom of the oven during baking. You can bake Lappish cheese in the oven, grill or hot electric oven. Turn when the surface gets brown and bake the other side until it looks similar.

**How to serve e.g.**
Have 50-100 g cheese and a tablespoon honey for each person. Tear the cheese into pieces and place in a cup filled with hot coffee. The cheese should be eaten when it is warm and soft. Honey can be used in coffee instead of sugar.

## THOROUGHLY SALTED MEAT À LA HULLU PORO

Put a grating at the bottom of a dish and place kitchen towels on top. Put a thick layer of coarse salt onto the paper and 2-3 kg boneless meat (in one piece) on top. Entirely cover the meat with coarse salt. Let the meat be in salt for 2-3 days depending on the size of the meat. Eat as cold cuts.

## REINDEER'S LIVER AND BOLETUS SAUSAGES

*1 kg broken barley*

*3 kg minced reindeer liver*

*4 dl syrup*

*5 dl chopped onion*

*8 dl chopped mushrooms*

*1 l milk*

*white pepper*

*salt*

*3 dl melted pork fat*

*intestines*

Cook the barleygrits. Melt the pork fat and lightly brown onions and mushrooms. Mix all ingredients with the cooked barleygrits and season the mixture with white pepper and salt. Fill the intestines with the substance with the help of a piping bag. Tie the sausages about 15 cm long, leave room for swelling. Use large amount of water or steam for boiling. Prick the sausages with a sharp stick after they have boiled for a couple of minutes. Let the sausages boil until tender. Fry the sausages with butter and syrup until the surface is crispy.

## TONGUE AND LIVER WITH MARINATED MUSTARD SAUCE

*(4 servings)*

*160 g beef tongue*

*160 g beef liver*

**Mustard sauce:**

*2 egg yolks*

*1 dl mustard*

*1 dl oil*

*1 tablespoon balsam vinegar*

*salt*

*white pepper*

*about 1 dl orange juice*

Cook the beef tongue for about one hour. Chill, and remove skin. Cut the liver into slices and slightly fry in butter. Roll the slices in coarse, grated pepper.

**Mustard Sauce:**
Put yolks, spices and mustard in a bowl, carefully stir in oil. Last add orange juice and vinegar. Spread sauce on a serving dish, place the tongue- and liver-slices on top and decorate e.g. with thyme.

## CLOUDBERRY FOOL

*1 l water*

*5 dl cloudberries*

*2 dl sugar*

*3 tablespoons potato flour*

Put the berries into cold water. Boil 4 dl berries until they turn into juice. Season the liquid with sugar. Thicken the juice with potato flour mixed with cold water. Add the remaining berries (frozen berries to the hot fool, fresh ones to the chilled fool).

## REINDEER BLOOD SAUSAGES

| |
|---|
| 7 dl blood |
| 3 dl beer |
| 100-150 g fat from entrails or small pieces of fat |
| 2 onions |
| 50 g butter |
| 1.3-1.5 dl barleyflour |
| 1.3-1.5 dl ryeflour |
| 2 teaspoons salt |
| white pepper |
| 4 m sausage skin |

Add flour to the blood, beat well and let stay for a while. Chop the onions, fry in butter and let cool. Add onions, fat and spices. Fill the sausage skins, leave room (about 1/3) for swelling. Tie the sausages. Let the sausages simmer at medium heat in salty water for about one hour. Water may not boil. Prick the sausages with a sharp stick after they have boiled for a couple of minutes and in between. Fry the sausages with butter until the surface is crispy.

## MELTED BUTTER-ONION SAUCE

| |
|---|
| 100 g butter |
| 200 g onions |
| 3 dl water |
| 1 teaspoon barley starch |
| water |

Chop the onions and fry in butter until golden yellow. Add the water and boil for one minute. Thicken with barley starch. Season with salt. Decorate the sauce with chives or onion sprouts in the summer.

## CARROT-LINGONBERRY COMPOTE

| |
|---|
| 1 dl lingonberries |
| 4 dl grated carrots |
| 3 dl sugar |
| 1 teaspoon red melantine |

Boil the lingonberries until they break. Add sugar and grated carrots. Mix melantine with a drop of water and add to the mixture. Boil for a couple of minutes and remove the scum from the surface. Pack at once into clean tins and close them immediately.

## KAMPSUT (BLOOD PATTIES)

| **Batter:** |
|---|
| 1 l water |
| 1 l blood |
| rye- or barley flour |
| fat from entrails or small pieces of fat |
| onion, marjoram, salt |

Make a thick batter. Bake cakes and boil them in salty water until tender.

*Delicious smell arises from the smoked reindeer roast, reindeer's liver and boletus sausages, blood sausages and 'kampsut'. Above 'luikut' (marrow) and on the right Lappish cheese and fried reindeer.*

# FEBRUARY

*The landscape is covered with cotton candy. Snow keeps on falling, reaching window sills, covering garden gates and fences. Sometimes there are flurries or snow is fluttering down, sometimes snow, chased by furious northern winds, lashes against windows.*

*Birches in the north, heavily loaded with snow, are bending down gracefully. Ice frosted trees standing along the river construct a filigree pattern.*

*Thickly covered by snow, nature takes its rest. For people working in the tourism branch it's time to wake up. For them the ice is breaking at this time of the year and piles of unpaid bills are reducing as visitors from all parts of the world are arriving. Meals and beverages are served, a joyous mood is spreading and everybody is happy.*

*Let's welcome the season!*

GARDEN ANGELICA SOUP . . . . . . . . . . . . 16

BUTTER PORRIDGE . . . . . . . . . . . . . . . . 16

LINGONBERRY SOUP . . . . . . . . . . . . . . . 16

OATMEAL BREAD . . . . . . . . . . . . . . . . . 16

STUFFED BREAST OF WILLOW GROUSE . . . . 17

SNOW EGGS . . . . . . . . . . . . . . . . . . . . 18

'LUIKUT' (MARROW) . . . . . . . . . . . . . . . 18

REINDEER BACK BROTH . . . . . . . . . . . . . 18

MERINGUE WILLOW GROUSE . . . . . . . . . . 18

*Garden angelica (angelica archangelica)*

## GARDEN ANGELICA SOUP

4 l stock of reindeer bones

(or other bouillon)

160 g wheat flour

3 dl double cream

500 g parboiled stems and
leaves of garden angelica

salt, white pepper

Let the butter melt in a saucepan. Add the wheat flour and allow to stew a little while in fat. Add the boiling stock in small batches mixing well at the same time. Let simmer 20 minutes in low heat. Stir in the 3-5 minutes parboiled stems of garden angelica that have been either chopped or ground in a mincing machine or in a blender. Add cream and season with salt and white pepper.

## BUTTER PORRIDGE

1-1.5 l milk

120 g butter

3 dl wheat flour

Melt the butter in a saucepan and mix with the wheat flour. Stir in the hot milk in small batches to the mixture. Let the porridge stew for about 10 minutes. Season with vanilla sugar or cardamom. Serve with lingonberry soup.

## LINGONBERRY SOUP

1 l lingonberries

300 g sugar

2 l water

2 dl potato flour

Boil the lingonberries, sugar and water until the berries break. At this stage lingonberries can be strained. Thicken the soup with potato flour mixed in a little cold water.

## OATMEAL BREAD

1 l sour milk

200 g oatgrains

about 1.8 kg wheat flour

50 g yeast

Add yeast and oatgrains to warm water and let dissolve for a couple of hours. Add flour beating well until the dough comes away from the dish and hands. Let the dough swell for about an hour. Make bread and bake. Oven temperature 200 centigrades. Baking time 20-30 minutes.

## STUFFED BREAST OF WILLOW GROUSE

*(4 servings)*

*2 willow grouses*

**minced willow grouse:**

*wing- and leg meat of a willow grouse*

*1 dl cream*

*2 egg yolks*

*juniper berries, salt, pepper*

Grind the breast- and wing meat of the willow grouse in a blender. Add cream and yolks and season with juniper berries. Make a soft meatloaf with the leg meat, yolks and cream. Remove the bones from the breastpiece and cut a pocket in the middle covering the entire breast. Pipe the pocket full of minced willow grouse. Brown it beautifully in a frying pan. Stew in earthenware in the oven under a foil until tender. Mix crushed cranberries and cream to stewing stock. Strain. Thicken slightly with barley starch. Check the taste. Cut the breast into about 1.5 cm thick slices and serve with sauce. You can use minced willow grouse e.g. as a ge-latinized appetizer, on toast or on morelbed. If you remove all bones from the willow grouse you can stuff it with meatloaf. A stuffed willow grouse breast dish can be decorated with petals of willowherb in the summer or with parsley and lingonberries in the winter.

*A stuffed willow grouse breast dish can be decorated with petals of willowherb in the summer or with parsley and lingonberries in the winter.*

## SNOW EGGS

Lift snow eggs with a big spoon from a meringue-dish to boiling milk. Boil until snow eggs ripen (about 3 minutes). Lift them to kitchen towels or gauze to drain. Snow eggs can also be made by lifting the rosettes to a plate and by ripening them in an microwave oven (30 sec. with full power). Serve e.g. with lingonberry- or cloudberry sauce.

## LUIKUT (MARROW)

| 2 kg reindeer thighbones in pieces of about 12 cm |
| 1 dl butter |
| 1 l water |
| salt, thyme |

Saw the thighbones from both ends, brown in butter in a frying pan and boil in water seasoned with salt and thyme until tender (about an hour). Remove the core from the inside and put on rye bread. Delicious as a snack or in a picnic lunchbox on a campfire or in a hut.

## REINDEER BACK BROTH

| 1 kg meaty reindeer back |
| 2 1/2 l water |
| 6 whole allspices |
| 6 white pepper corns |
| 2 carrots |
| 2 onions |
| 1 Swedish turnip |
| salt |

Put the meat into cold water in big chunks and heat to boiling point. Remove the scum from the surface of the stock and let the meat simmer slowly - about 3 hours or more - the longer boiling time the better broth. Add the spices before the meat is done. Keep the lid on the saucepan. Add the chopped potherbs and let the broth simmer until ready. If needed add a little water. Check the taste. Reindeer back broth can be served as a simple feast dinner.

## MERINGUE WILLOW GROUSE

| Vanilla ice-cream |

| **Meringue:** |
| 2 dl egg-white |
| 4 dl granulated sugar |
| a few drops lemon juice |

| **Lingonberry sauce:** |
| 1 l crushed lingonberries |
| 3 dl sugar |
| 1 dl berry liqueur |

Make meringue by beating egg-whites stiff and adding sugar in three batches. Pipe neck, wings and tail for the willow grouse of meringue and bake them until white. Make lingonberry sauce by cooking lingonberries.

*Snow egg and lingonberry sauce, above willow grouse made of meringue with parfait of an annual new shoot of spruce inside. In front lingonberry cream pudding, carrot oatmeal-chips, butter porridge and lingonberry soup.*

# march

The whiteness of the frozen snow scintillates in the glaring of the sun. In the restaurants next to the slopes, steaming hot meals and grog beverages are prepared. People are skiing. A cross-country ski run invites skiers to go on a tour into the vast nature.

The rucksack filled with a thermos, some round flat loaf and dried reindeer meat ensures a pleasant day. The snow white riverbed is lined with hundreds of snowmobile tracks. Dusk is falling. A burbot brought home from ice-hole fishing has been placed on the kitchen table.

POTATO PORRIDGE . . . . . . . . . . . . . . . . . 22

BARLEY FLOUR BREAD . . . . . . . . . . . . . 22

SOUR MILK BREAD . . . . . . . . . . . . . . . . 22

BURBOT ROE AND
LIVER WITH BUTTER . . . . . . . . . . . . . . . 22

ESCALOPE À LA HULLU PORO . . . . . . . . . 22

LOVE GRUEL . . . . . . . . . . . . . . . . . . . . 24

DRIED MEAT . . . . . . . . . . . . . . . . . . . . 24

DRY MEAT BROTH . . . . . . . . . . . . . . . . 24

RAW WHITEFISH WITH
BLUEBERRY SEASONING . . . . . . . . . . . . . 24

LINGONBERRY SNOW ON RYE DELICACY . . 24

LAPPISH HUT ROAST . . . . . . . . . . . . . . . 25

## POTATO PORRIDGE

1 l water

about 700 g potatoes

2 dl barley flour

Wash the potatoes and cook them until soft. Mash and add the boiling water. Let the porridge boil again and stir in the flour in small batches. Let it simmer about 1/2 hour. Season with salt and serve warm. Add a knob butter and milk on serving.

## BARLEY FLOUR BREAD

1 l cold water

less than one tablespoon salt

about 2 kg barley flour

wheat flour for baking

Knead the flour to cold salty water. Divide the dough into six. Tap round half a cm thick breads with the help of your knuckles. Use wheat flour as help. Prick the breads with a fork. Bake one minute in good oven temperature (over 300 centigrades).

## SOUR MILK BREAD

1 l sour milk

about 1 kg barley flour

25 g yeast

1 tablespoon salt

Add salt, yeast and flour to sour milk until the mixture is like gruel. Knead the dough with barley flour and roll about 2 cm thick pieces. Prick the breads before you put them into the oven. Bake until the breads turn brown. The oven temperature has to be 250 centigrades.

## BURBOT ROE AND LIVER WITH BUTTER

250 g fresh or frozen roe

1 teaspoon salt

1 small onion

100 g boiled burbot liver

Cleanse the tissues off the roe and whisk with a fork to get all the tissues and veins away. Add salt and let stay in salt for a couple of hours. Mash the boiled livers with a fork. Serve with dark fresh bread or use our march barley bread.

## ESCALOPE À LA HULLU PORO

500 g tenderloin beef

wheat flour for kneading

**Filling:**

2 small onions

60 g blue cheese

1/2 jar sour cream

100 g chopped smoked reindeer

black pepper

Mix the ingredients of the filling and take to a cool place. Divide the tenderloin into four parts and pound them to thin escalopes. Stuff with the filling. Fasten the edges of the escalope pockets, sprinkle with flour and fry until golden brown in medium heat. If you want sauce add 1 dl cream. Serve with lingonberries and pickled cucumbers.

*Dried meat, burbot roe and liver with barley bread, love gruel and Lappish cheese in coffee dish*

## LOVE GRUEL

| |
|---|
| *0.7 dl porridge rice* |
| *2 dl water* |
| *8 dl milk* |
| *1 dl raisins* |
| *2-3 tablespoons syrup* |
| *1/2 teaspoon salt* |
| *300-400 g Lappish cheese* |

Add rice to the boiling water. When water has been absorbed add the milk. Allow to simmer until tender (about 30 minutes). Add the syrup, salt, washed and if needed dissolved raisins and cubes of Lappish cheese when the gruel is ready. Let it stand warm for a while to give time for the cheese cubes to soften before serving.

## DRIED MEAT

4 cm thick meat pieces (reindeer, beef or elk) slightly and keep in room temperature for 3-4 days. Take to the roof of an outbuilding (to a rack specially made for that purpose) or wall to dry. Meat may dry for 3-4 weeks depending on the weather. Will be eaten as cold cut or as thin slices cut with a knife as a simple delicacy.

## DRY MEAT BROTH

| |
|---|
| *400 g bony drymeat* |
| *350 g potatoes* |
| *1 dl barley groats* |
| *1 onion* |

Let drymeat and barley grains dissolve separately overnight. If the meat is very salty change the water in between. Boil the meat and onion the following day and remove the scum. When the pieces of meat are nearly tender add barley grains. Let boil about 20 minutes. Stir in the potato cubes and check the taste.

## RAW WHITEFISH WITH BLUEBERRY SEASONING

| |
|---|
| *400 g whitefish* |
| *12 g onion* |
| *0.5 dl coarse ground allspices* |
| *4 teaspoons crushed blueberries* |
| *dill, coarse salt, a little sugar, special 'puikula' potatoes grown in Lapland* |

Raw-spice the whitefish fillets. Sprinkle a little sugar and crushed blueberries on top. Scratch the biggest salt junks away the next day. Cut thin slices and make a form of a fillet. Spread the crushed allspices underneath and chopped onion on top. Put a light weight on top. Can be eaten the next day with e.g. the special Lappish potatoes and dill.

## LINGONBERRY SNOW ON RYE DELICACY

| |
|---|
| *1/2 fresh rye bread* |
| *2 dl sugar* |
| *3 dl cream* |
| *1 dl crushed lingonberries* |
| *1/2 dl lingonberry liqueur* |
| *(Frozen lingonberries and rye breadcrumbs for decoration)* |

Grate fresh rye bread with a coarse grater. Spread granular sugar in a flat frying pan and the grated bread on top. Brown by stirring lightly with a wooden spatula. Beat the cream (leave a couple of dabs separately for decoration) and add the crushed lingonberries and a little lingonberry liqueur. Turn over the rye breadcrumbs on a round serving tray to a smooth layer and pipe the lingonberry snow on top. Decorate with whipped cream, lingonberries and some rye breadcrumbs.

## Lappish hut roast

*(Creamy sauce seasoned with juniper berries, braised campfire potatoes)*

### Reindeer roast

Salt a whole or boneless reindeer roast lightly overnight. Hang it on top of the hut near a fire. Small fires continue in the hut about 3 hours. You can make oven roast, sauteed reindeer or steak of reindeer roast.

### Sauce:

4 dl gravy

1 tablespoon mustard

2 dl double cream

50 g butter

2 tablespoons wheat flour

2 onions

6 juniper berries

Roll crushed juniper berries, mustard and pieces of onion in butter. Stir in the flour and mix. Add the gravy and let boil about 20 minutes. Strain and stir in cream and a dash of gin.

### Campfire potatoes:

Wash the potatoes well and wrap in foil. Put them on the edge of fire and turn from time to time.

*Reindeer roast.*

# APRIL

The sun in spring sheds its golden light on the landscape. Soon the snow will be gone. First there's only a small spot free of snow, soon a second and third will follow.

Winter is over. Sounds of spring arise from the breaking ice of the rivers. Again it's time for the savoury juniper plant. In earlier times it has also been used for healing purposes, especially for children when they had tooth-aches. Today it is used for decorating elk-roast and also for preparing desserts. Vitamins are important after the long time of winter.

Now, days are getting longer, the sun is out and people get a nice tan. The people's mood brightens up, cheeks are turning red, jackets and fur coats are getting too warm. There's no need to wear a cap for skiing – tiny drops of sweat appear on the forehead.

SOUR WHEAT BREAD . . . . . . . . . . . . . . . . . 28

BIRCH SAP &
CLOUDBERRY FOOL . . . . . . . . . . . . . . . . . 28

BERRY-RYE FLOUR PORRIDGE . . . . . . . . . 28

RAW-SPICED TROUT . . . . . . . . . . . . . . . . . 28

BOLETUS STEW . . . . . . . . . . . . . . . . . . . . 28

SMOKED TROUT . . . . . . . . . . . . . . . . . . . 29

THOROUGHLY
SALTED ELK OR
REINDEER ROAST . . . . . . . . . . . . . . . . . 29

CROWBERRY PARFAIT . . . . . . . . . . . . . . . 29

## SOUR WHEAT BREAD

25 g yeast

3 dl warm water

3 dl wheat or graham flour

Mix yeast, water and flour. Cover the dough with cloth. Keep in room temperature until the following day.

7 dl water

1 tablespoon salt

1 tablespoon oil

about 2.3 l wheat flour

Add the water, salt, oil and flour the following day. Let the dough rise for about an hour. Bake two loaves and let them rise still half an hour on a baking sheet. If you prefer a crispier crust brush the loaves with water and should you prefer soft crust brush with sour milk. Make cuts on the surface. Bake 45 minutes in 200 centigrades.

## BIRCH SAP & CLOUDBERRY FOOL

1 l birch saps

about 1/2 l cloudberries

3 tablespoons potato flour

1 dl honey

Put the cloudberries into cold water. Boil part of the berries until they break. Flavour with honey and thicken with potato flour mixed with cold water. Add the remaining frozen berries to the hot fool. If the berries are fresh add them to cold fool.

## BERRY-RYE FLOUR PORRIDGE

2 l water

1/2 l berries, e.g. blueberries or lingonberries

1 1/2 dl sugar

4-5 dl rye flour

1-2 tablespoons potato flour

2 tablespoons syrup

1 teaspoon salt

Crush the rinsed berries and bring them to a quick boil in water seasoned with salt and sugar. Fold rye flour little by little beating strongly. Porridge may simmer about an hour during which time it must be mixed frequently.

Thicken the porridge finally with potato flour mixed in a little amount of cold water. It may still boil up after which it will be flavoured with syrup. Pour the porridge into a dish, add sugar and serve cold.

## RAW-SPICED TROUT

500 g trout or rainbow trout

250 g onion, celery, carrot, coarse salt and leek honey, black pepper

herbs, e.g. thyme, sage, basil or chervil

Grate the vegetables, chop the spices and combine with salt. Place the trouts in a dish skin-side down. Cover with grated and spiced mixture. Allow to marinate overnight. The following day cut the fish into thin slices and serve.

## BOLETUS STEW

500 g fresh boletus or

1 dl dried boletus

1 onion

2 dl cream

50 g butter

*2 tablespoons wheat flour*

*parsley, vegetable stock, thyme*

*(port wine)*

Melt the butter in a saucepan. Roll the mashed boletus in butter. Add wheat flour, vegetable stock and cream. Cook about 10 minutes. Add chopped parsley, thyme and finally port wine (if available). Serve with special Lappish potatoes.

## SMOKED TROUT

*1 trout weighing 2 kg*

*alder chips*

*4 lumps of sugar*

*juniper sprig*

Put the alder chips, juniper sprig and lumps of sugar on the bottom of a smoke oven. (Sugar gives a beautiful colour). Place the fish into smoke oven, first higher heat to make the colour beautiful, then lower heat, where the fish may be smoked about half an hour. The fish is tender when the fins and bones come loose when the fish is lifted. Salt the smoked fish by watering it for a short while with strong coarse salt water.

## THOROUGHLY SALTED ELK OR REINDEER ROAST

*large elk roast*

*coarse salt*

Wrap a frozen elk roast in greaseproof paper and place into a large wooden receptacle, inside coarse salt so that there is about 10 cm salt on every side. Let it remain in salt for 2-3 months. To be used as cold cuts or dissolved in food preparation.

## CROWBERRY PARFAIT

*(serves 4)*

*6 egg yolks*

*1 dl water*

*100 g icing sugar*

*150 g sugar*

*5 dl double cream*

*1-2 dl crowberry juice*

Beat together the cream and icing sugar. Cream the yolks. Add the boiling sugar water to cream. Whip the mixture constantly. Cool the mixture quickly e.g. on ice cubes whipping from time to time. Add crowberry juice to cold mixture to taste. Stir in the whipped cream. Freeze parfait quickly in dessert dishes.

# MAY

The ground turns brown, soon new and fresh plants will grow. The sun is warming up the frozen ground and before long the ice on the rivers will be gone. Now as rivers are free of ice, it is time to sow.

It's also time to clear the store rooms, soon they will be filled again. A farewell ceremony for skiers takes place on Mother's day. For a last time in the season ski-lifts are carrying skiers uphill to a slope covered with artificial snow. The birch is the plant of the month, its fresh leaves and buds have traditionally been used to cure high blood pressure. People throughout the world know to appreciate the plant which is also used for rheumatism, and tea made from birch leaves is popular. The most delicious beverage 'magic sima' - birch sap mead - is made from birch saps in spring.

SLIGHTLY SALTED REINDEER FILLET ...... 32

TENORIVER SALMON
WITH TWO SAUCES ................... 32

BROWN BREAD ..................... 32

SPRING PORRIDGE .................. 34

BEET-BARLEY GRAIN-CASSEROLE ........ 34

BIRCH SAP MEAD ................. 34

RHUBARB-PIE ...................... 34

MARINATED BERRIES
IN HONEY CREAM ................... 34

## SLIGHTLY SALTED REINDEER FILLET

*300 g tenderloin reindeer*

*coarse salt, crushed black pepper*

Spread a little coarse salt on the bottom of the dish. Place the reindeer fillet on the salt. Sprinkle some more salt and crushed black pepper on top. Put a weight on and leave for about a day.

## TENORIVER SALMON WITH TWO SAUCES

*(Cloudberry sauce and birch-bud sauce)*

Fry the fresh salmon slices until nicely brown. Season with crushed white pepper and salt. Boil quickly in a little white wine. Serve with fresh vegetables, cloudberry- and birch-bud sauce (cold or warm) and dill-potatoes.

### Cloudberry sauce

*30 g butter*

*30 g wheat flour*

*4 dl cloudberry liqueur*

*white pepper from mill*

*black pepper from mill*

*coarse salt*

*1 dl crushed cloudberries, honey*

Melt the butter and add the wheat flour, but do not brown. Stir in the fish stock. Boil for five minutes. Add the cloudberry liqueur and spices. Boil another five minutes. Stir in the crushed cloudberries and honey last. Check the taste.

### Cold birch-bud sauce

*40 g butter*

*wheat flour*

*2 dl fish stock*

*1/2 dl birch-buds*

*3 tablespoons unripened cheese*

Put the buds, honey and unripened cheese to a blender. Mix until the compound is smooth. Stir in the double cream and continue to stir for a couple of minutes.

### Warm birch-bud sauce

*100 g birch-buds*

*100 g grated carrots*

*100 g grated celery*

*100 g grated potatoes*

*100 g chopped onions*

*0.7 dl fish stock*

*2 dl cream*

*white wine*

*chopped dill*

Roll the potherbs quickly in butter, braise in fish stock and liquidize. Add the cream, chopped dill and birch-buds. If required thicken with a little wheat flour. Season finally with a little white wine.

## BROWN BREAD

**Sourdough:**

*5 dl water*

*3 dl rye porridge flour*

**Dough:**

*4 dl water*

*50 g yeast*

| 2 teaspoons salt |
| 12 dl wheat flour |
| 3 dl rye flour |

Boil water quickly and pour on the rye flour. Blend. Cover with oven wrap and leave in room temperature until next day. Pour handwarm water over the sourdough. Stir in the crumbled yeast. Add salt and flour. The dough should not be too soft. Therefore add a couple dl wheat flour if required. Let the dough rise for an hour. Knead smooth and divide into two. Sprinkle two baskets with flour or cover two long moulds with greaseproof paper. Put the dough into baskets or moulds, cover with cloth and let rise for about an hour. Tip the basket bread on greaseproof paper or bake the bread in their moulds at 175 centigrades for about an hour.

*Smoked trout, Tenoriver salmon with two sauces, Lappish potatoes and slightly salted reindeer fillet.*

## SPRING PORRIDGE

*1 1/2 cups oatgrains or rye flakes*

*1/2 kg fresh rhubarb*

*1 l water*

*little salt*

Put the oatgrains with rhubarb pieces into cold water and boil until tender. Season with salt. Serve either warm or cold, with or without milk.

## BEET-BARLEY GRAIN-CASSEROLE

Stir cooked and crushed or raw, grated beet to the leftovers from the barley grain porridge. Season with salt. Grease a mould. Put the mixture into the mould. Sprinkle butter dabs on top and bake in 180 centigrades for about an hour.

## BIRCH SAP MEAD

*4 l birch sap*

*1/2 kg sugar*

*1 lemon*

*1/8 teaspoon yeast*

*raisins, sugar*

Dissolve the sugar with boiling water. Peel the lemon and remove the white part of the peels. Cut the lemon into slices and remove seeds. Pour the boiling sugar water over lemon slices and peels. Stir in yeast dissolved in a small amount of mead when the mixture has cooled. Mead may ferment until foam rises on the surface. Strain the mead and bottle. Put first a couple of raisins and a teaspoon sugar into each bottle. Close the bottle well and preserve them in a cool place. Mead is ready in a week's time.

## RHUBARB-PIE

*1 l rhubarb pieces*

*200 g sugar*

*200 g wheat flour*

*200 g butter*

Blend wheat flour well with sugar and put on an oven sheet. Place rhubarb pieces on top, slice cold butter with a cheese slicer and place on top of the pie to cover the surface completely. Bake in 200 centigrades for about 20-30 minutes. Delicious e.g. with vanilla ice cream.

## MARINATED BERRIES IN HONEY CREAM

*1 dl raspberries*

*1 dl cloudberries*

*1 dl blueberries*

*1 dl lingonberries*

*4 dl cream*

*5 dl berry liqueur*

*2 dl sugar juice*

Place the berries in their own bowls. Pour juice containing liqueur and sugar juice into each bowl and leave to marinate overnight. Serve in a high glass or a bowl. Beat the cream. Season with honey which crowns the marinated berries.

# JUNE

J une - nature is awakening. Birchbuds open, tips of firs, sprouts of stinging nettle and birch sap can be harvested. At first colours are pale green.

Then, all of a sudden it's summer and soon it is possible to bind fresh twigs into a besom. Dandelions are competing with the yellow colour of the sun. Let's welcome life and summer!

The fishermen's rucksack is getting heavier and heavier. Fish is now part of the daily menu. The herb of the month is the stinging nettle. Its fresh leaves are delicious in salads or soups. The nettle is extremely rich in minerals and vitamins. It is even used as a medicinal plant for diabetes and anaemia.

SALMON IN LINGONBERRY SAUCE  . . . . . . 38

PRETZEL-SHAPED SUMMER BUNS  . . . . . . . 38

PERCH FILLETS
WITH DANDELION SAUCE . . . . . . . . . . . . . 38

BREAD SOUP  . . . . . . . . . . . . . . . . . . . . . 40

GARDEN ANGELICA JUICE . . . . . . . . . . . 40

NETTLE SOUP  . . . . . . . . . . . . . . . . . . . . 40

SALMON SOUP  . . . . . . . . . . . . . . . . . . . 40

UNRIPENED CHEESE PUDDING  . . . . . . . . 40

SPRUCE SHOOTS JAM  . . . . . . . . . . . . . . . 41

## SALMON IN LINGONBERRY SAUCE

*(4 servings)*

*750 g salmon*

**Sauce:**

*3 dl lingonberries*

*1 dl sugar*

*1 dl water*

*1 dl chopped dill*

*1 l fish stock*

*4 cl lingonberry liqueur*

*3 dl double cream*

*butter, wheat flour*

Boil lingonberries in sugar water until they break. Strain. Melt the butter and add the wheat flour. Season lingonberry soup with fish stock. Stir in chopped dill and cream. Boil quickly. Divide the salmon into four. Fry in a lot of butter (the fish-side down). Place the fried fish on sauce and serve the fish and sauce separately.

## PRETZEL-SHAPED SUMMER BUNS

*1 l sour milk*

*1 kg sugar*

*1 kg butter*

*about 1.5 kg wheat flour*

*4 teaspoons soda*

*4 teaspoons baking flour*

Beat sugar and butter. Add the sour milk, soda and wheat flour. Knead dough until as soft as possible. Bake a stick as thick as a finger and cut it into 10 cm long pieces. Make them pretzel-shaped and bake in 250 centigrades until golden brown.

## PERCH FILLETS WITH DANDELION SAUCE

*(4 servings)*

*600 g perch fillets*

*salt*

*wheat flour*

*butter for frying*

Roll the fillets in a mixture of salt and wheat flour. Fry both sides in butter for a couple of minutes.

**Dandelion sauce:**

*3 dl dandelion leaves*

*2 dl chives*

*2 dl cream*

*3 dl fish stock*

*40 g butter*

*2 tablespoons barley starch*

*salt, black pepper*

Chop the dandelion leaves and chives. Fry in butter and add the fish stock. Simmer for about five minutes. Stir in cream to taste and thicken with barley starch if needed.

*Salmon in lingonberry sauce, cucumber-herb spread, salmon soup (page 40) and perch fillets*

## BREAD SOUP

300 g hard dark bread cubes

2 l milk

Heat the milk and stir in the bread cubes. Serve with butter and sugar.

## GARDEN ANGELICA JUICE

6 l water

2 kg sugar

3 kg garden angelica

40 g citric or tartaric acid

Wash and chop the garden angelica. Let stand in cold water for three days and strain. Add the sugar and citric acid last.

## NETTLE SOUP

1/2 l milk

2 dl cream

3 dl vegetable stock

40 g wheat flour

40 g butter

100 g parboiled nettles

salt

Chop the nettles and fry in butter. Add the wheat flour, vegetable stock and allow to simmer for about five minutes. Stir in the milk last and add cream for a better taste. Season finally with salt.

## SALMON SOUP

400 g salmon cubes

600 g potatoes (equal chunks)

2 onions

allspice, white pepper, fish stock powder

(rather fish stock out of boiled fish bones, in which case reduce the amount of water)

50 g butter

1/2 l water

1 l milk

1 dl cream

dill

Let the potatoes and onion pieces boil until medium tender in stock seasoned with peppers. Stir in the salmon cubes and milk. Let simmer slowly until tender. Add the milk and a butter dab. Check the taste and garnish with chopped dill.

## UNRIPENED CHEESE PUDDING

1 dl sugar

1 dl cream (whipped)

200 g bel ami unripened cheese

1 teaspoon vanilla sugar

4 gelatines

Dissolve the gelatines, beat the cream and stir in the unripened cheese, whipped cream and sugar. Add the dissolved and drained gelatines and place in serving bowls.

# SPRUCE SHOOTS JAM

5-6 l spruce shoots

1 kg sugar

gelatine

Dissolve the spruce shoots in cold water overnight. Enough water is needed to cover the shoots. Cook them the following day in dissolving water for about two hours. Strain and add the sugar. Boil another two hours stirring from time to time. Add the gelatine to the reddish brown liquid.

*Rhubarb-pie, garden angelica juice, birch sap mead, garden angelica-pie*

# july

*L* ife in summer is beyond compare. Meadows
are blue, yellow, red and white. Gardeners
*make use of the long days and the nightless nights.*
*Nowhere, except at the polar circle, herbs such as*
*tarragon, parsley or basil are of such pleasant*
*taste. Fish, salad, vegetables and berries are typical*
*for this time of the year.*
*Angelica is the plant of the month. In Lapland and*
*in Greenland it is used as a medicinal plant and for*
*eating. When used as a medicinal plant, it can be*
*used for cramps, cough and sore throat. It*
*is also a plant for lovers as it is said to*
*stimulate fertility.*

RICE PORRIDGE COVERED
WITH DRYMEAT . . . . . . . . . . . . . . . . . . 44

BLACKCURRANT-LEAF DRINK . . . . . . . . 44

GARDEN ANGELICA-PIE . . . . . . . . . . . . . 44

HORS-DŒVRE OF
THE SUMMER DELICACIES . . . . . . . . . . . . 44

RHUBARB SKIM . . . . . . . . . . . . . . . . . . . 44

SALMON AND REINDEER
WITH TWO SAUCES . . . . . . . . . . . . . . . . . 45

MOREL SAUCE FOR REINDEER . . . . . . . . . 45

LINGONBERRY SAUCE FOR THE FISH . . . . . 45

CUCUMBER-HERB SPREAD . . . . . . . . . . . . 46

CAKES À LA TAIVAANVALKEAT . . . . . . . . 46

## RICE PORRIDGE COVERED WITH DRYMEAT

2 dl rice

1 l milk

2 tablespoons butter

1/2 tablespoon salt

Boil the porridge or let it simmer in the oven. If made in the oven the simmering time is about an hour at 150 centigrades. It takes the same time if the porridge is boiled on the stove. Cut thin slices of dried meat on top of the tender porridge. Served in this way the porridge is an excellent lunch.

## BLACKCURRANT-LEAF DRINK

1/2 bucket blackcurrant-leaves

50 g tartaric acid

700 g sugar

7 l boiling water

Rinse the blackcurrant-leaves. Mix the tartaric acid and sugar with boiling water and pour the water over the leaves. Let stand a couple of days, strain and bottle. The beverage can be preserved in a cold place for a few weeks.

## GARDEN ANGELICA-PIE

### Bottom:

250 g butter

2 dl sugar

2 eggs

2.5 dl wheat flour

2.5 dl rye flour

1 teaspoon baking powder

Beat butter and sugar. Add the eggs one at a time. Sprinkle the flour containing baking powder. Spread on a greased baking sheet.

### Filling:

6 dl sour cream

3 eggs

1.5 dl sugar

3 tablespoons vanilla sugar

0.5-1 dl crushed garden angelica

Mix all ingredients gently and spread on top of the sponge. Bake for 40 minutes at 175 centigrades.

## HORS-D'ŒUVRE OF THE SUMMER DELICACIES

(4 servings)

12 new potatoes

150 g mushroom salad

150 g whitefish or pike roe

150 g dill-butter

Boil the potatoes until tender, chill, split and scoop out a little of the inside. Season the roe with salt and black pepper. Place six potato halves on top of a bed of lettuce in each portion. Fill two with mushroom salad, two with roe and onion and the remaining two with dill-butter. Garnish with fresh vegetables and herbs.

## RHUBARB SKIM

500 g rhubarb

2 dl sugar

*3 dl water*

*1 tablespoonful honey*

*2 egg-whites*

Chop the rhubarb and boil the pieces in water-sugar-mixture until tender. Chill and flavour with honey. Put the compound into an ice cream machine and add the yolks at last. If unavailable the sorbet can also be made with the help of a mixer and freezer. Put the rhubarb mixture in a bowl into the freezer and beat it from time to time until the ice ferns break. Add stiff beaten whites last. Chill. Before serving keep the bowl for ten minutes in room temperature. Serve as a snack or dessert.

## SALMON AND REINDEER WITH TWO SAUCES

*(4 servings)*

*500 g salmon*

*400 g salted reindeer fillet*

*crushed lingonberries*

*2 dl cream*

*2 dl beef stock*

*2 dl fish stock*

Brown the reindeer fillets in butter, rub the spices on the surface and let simmer in an oven until tender. Fry the salmon slices in a little butter.

## MOREL SAUCE FOR REINDEER

*50 g butter*

*1 big onion*

*100 g parboiled morels*

*2 tablespoons wheat flour*

*vegetable stock*

*crushed white pepper*

*(salt)*

*water*

*1 dl double cream*

*white wine*

Chop the morels and onion. Melt the butter in a saucepan. Add the onion with butter and fry them until golden brown. Stir in the morels and continue to simmer. Add the wheat flour

beating strongly. Add boiling water if required. Allow to thicken then and add vegetable stock, crushed white pepper and salt. Finally cream and a drop of wine. Check the taste.

## LINGONBERRY SAUCE FOR THE FISH

*1 tablespoon wheat flour*

*0.5 dl sugar*

*3 dl crushed lingonberries*

*1 onion*

*2 dl water*

*vegetable stock*

*1 tablespoon lingonberry liqueur*

*chopped dill, black and white pepper*

Quick boil the wheat flour, crushed lingonberries, water, onion and sugar. Break the mixture with a blender and strain. Season and improve taste with lingonberry liqueur and cream.

# CUCUMBER-HERB SPREAD

200 g unseasoned, unripened cheese

grated and drained cucumber

grated onions to taste

chopped herbs

pinch of salt

Mix the ingredients well and chill.

# CAKES À LA TAIVAANVALKEAT

### Sponge cake:

6 eggs

3.5 dl sugar

3.5 dl wheat flour

Beat the eggs and sugar. Filter in the wheat flour. Bake in a greased tin covered with bread-crumbs for 45 minutes at 180 centigrades.

### Chocolate base:

6 eggs

3.5 dl sugar

3.5 dl wheat flour

1.5 tablespoons cocoa powder

Make the same way as the sponge cake, but mix cocoa powder with the wheat flour.

### Meringue cake:

2 dl egg-white

4 dl sugar

a drop of lemon juice

Beat the egg-white and sugar. Add the sugar in three batches. Bake at 80-120 centigrades for about ten minutes.

### Fillings:

**Raspberry-curd cheese filling**
one jar curd cheese
2 dl cream
1/2 l raspberries
5 gelatines
Beat the cream and sugar. Add the raspberries and the dissolved, chilled gelatines last.

**Butter-cream**
3/4 dl sugar
3/4 dl water
200 butter
Boil the water and sugar. Chill and add the creamed butter. Flavour to taste e.g. with coffee or vanilla.

**Berry filling:**
Mix lightly the same quantity of cloudberries, raspberries and lingonberries. Season with sugar.

### Surface coatings:

**Jelly icing**
Decorate the cake with berries and set with juice.

**Chocolate icing:**
150 g dark baking chocolate
0.5 dl cream
Allow the chocolate to melt, add the cream and frost the cake.

**Butter icing:**
3/4 dl sugar
3/4 dl water
3 egg yolks
150-200 g unsalted butter
Boil the water and sugar. Add to the yolks in thin ribbons beating heavily all the time. Add the chilled mixture in small batches with the creamed butter beating heavily. Flavour the icing with coffee, cocoa, rum, liqueur etc.

*Wedding cake with different layers of forest berries. Cloudberry cake with butter icing on the left. On the right Mickey Mouse and in the middle a cherry flavoured Christmas cake. In front of the window Lappish woman's love-philtre.*

Kuva: Tapio Mäki

# AUGUST

Willowherbs are in bloom and days are getting shorter. Nature appears in various shades of violet and the dark green of the grass is like a sign showing that autumn will soon come. Still, the weather can change and surprise with a lot of sun and warm temperatures. Then, mosquitos can be seen again, celebrating in the evening sun.

It is time to pick berries and mushrooms. Buckets filled with cloudberries are sold to shops, soon they'll be on their way to the gourmets of the south. People cheer up seeing the enormous piles of cloudberries on the market.

Mushrooms will be dried and only the best will be eaten right away. 'Puikulas' the egg-shaped superb potatoes are harvested.

The plant of the month is the blackcurrant. It is also a medicinal plant, used to cure colds. Blackcurrant is rich in vitamins comparable to sea buckthorn. Its leaves, roots and twigs are used to ease pains of rheumatism or for high blood pressure. Blueberries are traditionally used as a medicinal cure for the stomach, they contain natural insulin.

A LAPPISH WOMEN'S LOVE-PHILTRE . . . . . . . . . . . . . . . . . . . . 50

BLUEBERRY PORRIDGE . . . . . . . . . . . . . . . 50

'PUIKULA' POTATOES IN FOIL . . . . . . . . . . 50

BOLETUS ROLLS . . . . . . . . . . . . . . . . . . . . 50

GELATINIZED REINDEER TONGUE . . . . . . . 50

BLUEBERRY-CLOUDBERRY FOOL . . . . . . . . 51

SALMON-WHITEFISH ROLL . . . . . . . . . . . . . 51

POTHERBS SAUCE . . . . . . . . . . . . . . . . . . . 51

SPRUCE SHOOT BUTTER . . . . . . . . . . . . . . 52

ROWAN BERRY WINE . . . . . . . . . . . . . . . 52

CLOUDBERRY PUDDING . . . . . . . . . . . . . . . 52

## a lappish women's love-philtre

*3 l water*

*4 cups blueberries*

*4 cups sugar*

Mix the ingredients. Let the mixture rest in a transparent glass jar on the window sill in the sun for three weeks. Bottle and keep in a cold place. To be drunk during the Christmas time.

## blueberry porridge

*1 l water*

*400 g blueberries*

*3 dl sugar*

*1 white bread loaf*

*butter for frying*

Boil the picked berries with sugar to a pulp. Cut the bread into thin slices and fry until golden brown. Place blueberry pulp on the bottom of a shallow dish and the brown bread slices on top. Cover with the pulp and serve medium warm with milk.

## different ways to prepare the lappish puikula potatoes

**'Puikula' potatoes in foil**
Wrap 'puikulas' in foil and put to oven or glowing embers. Leave there until tender. Make a couple of cm cuts into the foil and potato. Stuff the cuts e.g. with spiced butter or unripened cheese containing smoked reindeer, onion and chopped parsley. An alternative excellent filling is white pepper, onion, chopped dill and coldsmoked salmon into sour cream.

**Potatoes cooked over an open fire:**
Split small 'puikulas' with the peel on. Place them in a large frying pan next to each other on butter and spices, the split halves down. Let them cook over the open fire about ten minutes.

**Potatoes with melted butter:**
Rinse the 'puikulas' well but do not peel. Boil in low temperature or in a steamer. Eat with dill and melted butter.

## boletus rolls

*5 dl sour milk or yogurt*

*2 teaspoons herbal salt*

*50 g yeast*

*3-4 tablespoons honey*

*2 tablespoons oil*

*1 dl dried boletus*

*(or 400 g fresh)*

*1 dl sunflower seeds*

*6 dl graham flour*

*7-8 dl wheat flour*

*or yeastbread flour*

*egg for brushing*

Crumble the yeast in a bowl. Heat the sour milk and honey until handwarm. Stir in the oil, herbal salt, dissolved boletus and flour. Let rise about 40 minutes. Make two loaves and divide them into 12 pieces. Make rolls and let them rise for 30 minutes. Brush with an egg and bake for 15 minutes at 225 centigrades.

## gelatinized reindeer tongue

Reserve a whole reindeer tongue, fresh or

coldsmoked for each diner. Let the reindeer tongues simmer in low heat for one and a half hours or until softened. Remove the skins of the tongues and let cool in the boiling stock. Cut the chilled tongues into thin slices lengthways. Serve on a plate. Garnish and set either with gelatine made of stock, melted berry gelatine or spruce shoot gelatine depending on the combination of the meal. Serve gelatinized reindeer tongue with fresh salad and toast bread or mushrooms.

## BLUEBERRY-CLOUDBERRY FOOL

(4 servings)

0.7 l water

1/2 dl blueberries

1 dl sugar

2 tablespoons potato flour

3 dl cloudberries

Put the blueberries into cold water and boil until they turn into juice. Season the liquid with sugar. Thicken the juice with potato flour mixed with a little water and let the fool boil quickly. Add the remaining blueberries, cloud-

berries – frozen berries to the hot fool, fresh ones to the chilled fool. Pour in the serving dish, sprinkle a little sugar on top and leave to chill at room temperature. Serve with milk or whipped cream.

## SALMON-WHITEFISH ROLL

(4 servings)

2 whitefish fillets

2 salmon fillets

50 g butter

Pinch of white pepper

thyme

salt

Remove the fish skins. Mix the spices with soft butter. Place the butterspread between the fish fillets. Split the fillets lengthways and roll up. Fix the rolls with a stick and fry in the oven for about 20-25 minutes at 175 centigrades.

## POTHERBS SAUCE

1 carrot

1 parsnip

10 small radishes

1 broccoli

1 onion

50 g butter

1 dl cream

1 dl sour cream

fish stock

white pepper

(1-2 tablespoons wheat flour)

fresh lovage

Cube the potherbs. Melt the butter in a saucepan. Fry quickly all potherbs except broccoli for about five minutes. Stir in the fish stock. Simmer the potherbs until tender. Add the broccoli, cream and sour cream. Boil the sauce if it is not thick enough. Mix a little water with wheat flour and thicken the sauce. Boil and season to taste with salt and white pepper. Garnish with chopped fresh lovage.

## SPRUCE SHOOT BUTTER

| |
|---|
| *500 g butter* |
| *0.5 dl chopped spruce shoots* |
| *(fresh annual shoots)* |
| *2 tablespoons spruce shoot syrup* |
| *salt* |

Beat the butter until creamy and stir in the other ingredients. Let stand for one day before serving.

## ROWAN BERRY WINE

| |
|---|
| *6-8 kg rowan berries* |
| *0.5 kg sweet apples or raisins* |
| *0.5 kg blueberries* |
| *6.5 kg sugar* |
| *wine yeast (according to instructions)* |
| *nutrient salt (according to instructions)* |

Crush the rowan berries and pour boiling water over them. Let stand for an hour. Dissolve 4 kg sugar in hot water and pour into the vessel. Add cool water until the amount of liquid is 23 litres. Dissolve the nutrient salt in a glass of water and pour into the fermentation vessel. The liquid may not exceed 30 centigrades. Dissolve the wine yeast in a glass of water and let stand about ten minutes. Stir the yeast to the vessel and fix the fermentation lock when the temperature of the vessel is about 25 centigrades. Let stand for five days. Melt 2.5 kg sugar with water and chill the liquid. Add the chilled sugar-liquid to the fermentation vessel and shake. When the wine has fermented for 2-3 weeks and the water lock bubbles once per minute, the wine is ready. Strain and dissolve the stagnation agent in a glass of water and add to the fermentation vessel. Shake during 2-3 days. Dissolve the clarifier in a glass of water, stir into the fermentation vessel, shake and let stand for 3-4 days or as long the wine is clear. Bottle the wine into clean bottles.

## CLOUDBERRY PUDDING

| |
|---|
| *5 dl low-fat milk* |
| *3 dl cloudberries* |
| *200 g granular sugar* |
| *2 eggs* |
| *10 gelatines* |
| *5 dl double cream* |
| *1 dl cloudberries for decoration* |

Beat the sugar and eggs in a saucepan with a thick bottom. Add the milk. Heat slowly stirring constantly until the mixture thickens. You can do this also 'au bain-marie' (in a water bath). Stir in well dissolved and drained gelatines. Chill quickly e.g. on ice mixing constantly. Chill nearly to the freezing point. Stir in the mashed and strained cloudberries. Mix the soft whipped cream last. Pour the pudding in dishes and let set in a cold place. Tip to serving dishes: Garnish with cloudberries.

*Trout gets its flavour*
*from juniper and alder.*

# SEPTEMBER

The autumn with its stunning colours again attracts tourists. Shades of orange are colouring the landscape, it's time to harvest. Rowan twigs are bending under their heavy load. It's time to harvest the berries and to make wine from them.

Remaining potatoes and vegetables will be stored for the winter. Now the store rooms are filled again with preserves, juice and dried herbs.

In earlier times 'grain was filled into boxes, potatoes were thrown in a pit and women were locked in the house', this implying that women had to do a lot of work in the house at that time of the year. Then, men went to hunt bringing back poultry from the woods or fields.

Who goes hunting nowadays? Next to those tourists who are attracted by the colours of 'ruska' there is a so-called 'Euro-hunter'. A willow grouse or capercaille shot by the 'man from Brussels' is an incomparable delicacy for him.

KATEKEETA PUDDING . . . . . . . . . . . . . . . 56

CARROT-YEAST BREAD . . . . . . . . . . . . . . 56

MUSHROOM STEAKS . . . . . . . . . . . . . . . . 56

LINGONBERRY FOOL . . . . . . . . . . . . . . . . 56

CARROT TIMBALE . . . . . . . . . . . . . . . . . 56

SMOKED REINDEER
-MUSHROOM SOUP . . . . . . . . . . . . . . . . 57

SPRUCE SHOOT PARFAIT . . . . . . . . . . . . . 57

WOOD GROUSE ROAST . . . . . . . . . . . . . . 57

## KATEKEETA PUDDING

2 dl dried sour bread in small pieces

1/2 l blueberries

1 l water

2 tablespoons potato flour

Make a pudding with the ingredients. There may also be unbroken pieces of sour bread in the pudding. Eat with milk either warm or cold.

## CARROT-YEAST BREAD

50 g yeast

1 l milk

1 tablespoon salt

1/2 kg wheat flour

1/2 kg rye flour

1/2 kg barley flour

4 dl grated carrot

Dissolve the yeast in water and stir in lukewarm dough-liquid. Add the grated carrots and flour. Knead until the dough is soft and starts to crack. Sprinkle flour on the surface and let rise until double in size. Bake three round loaves on the table. Decorate with a pastry wheel. Let rise on a baking sheet for about 15 minutes under a cloth and bake in an oven for half an hour at 225 centigrades.

## MUSHROOM STEAKS

300 g parboiled mushrooms

5 potatoes

1 onion

40 g wheat flour

salt

1 egg

garlic

Mince the mushrooms and potatoes in a mincing machine. Stir in the other ingredients. Fry steaks in a pancake frying pan. Serve with lingonberries and sour cream.

## LINGONBERRY FOOL

1 l water

4.5 dl lingonberries

1 dl sugar

4 tablespoons potato flour

3 carrots

Put the lingonberries into cold water and boil until they become juice. Season with sugar. Thicken the juice with potato flour mixed with a little water and let the fool boil quickly. Add the grated carrot to the hot fool. Pour in serving dishes and sprinkle a little sugar on top. Serve with whipped cream.

## CARROT TIMBALE

(4 servings)

200 g carrots

(can be replaced by beets)

2 eggs

1 dl double cream

salt, pepper, a pinch of sugar

Cook the carrots. Strain. Mash with an egg and cream in a blender. Season with salt, pepper and sugar. Pour the mixture into greased timbale dishes and bake in the oven in a water bath 30-40 minutes at 175 centigrades. Let rest for five minutes before tipping.

## SMOKED REINDEER-MUSHROOM SOUP

100 g smoked reindeer

100 g parboiled mushrooms

1 onion

2 tablespoons butter

2 tablespoons wheat flour

2 dl cream

7 dl stock

black pepper

Chop the smoked reindeer, mushrooms and onion. Roll in butter in a sauce pan. Stir in the wheat flour and stock. Let simmer about ten minutes. Add the cream last. Boil quickly again and add black pepper. Be careful with salt, as smoked reindeer is salty!

## SPRUCE SHOOT PARFAIT

(4 servings)

6 egg yolks

150 g sugar

1 dl water

100 g icing sugar

5 dl double cream

2 dl spruce shoot syrup

Beat the cream and icing sugar. Beat the yolks until creamy. Add the boiling sugar water and beat. Chill the mixture quickly e.g. on ice and whip occasionally. Add spruce shoot syrup to taste to the mixture. Stir in the whipped cream. Chill the parfait quickly.

**Spruce shoot syrup**
Spruce shoot syrup is made by dissolving the shoots (the new light green annual growth of the spruce) in a cold place overnight. Boil them after that, e.g. 10 l shoots - 10 l water. In four hours the liquid is green. Add 2 kg sugar and let simmer until there is about 4 l mixture left and the syrup has turned rust-brown. If you want jelly stop boiling when there is 6 l of mixture left. Set with gelatine.

## WOOD GROUSE ROAST

1 wood grouse

pork fat (American bacon)

**Marinade:**

6 juniper berries

1 dl oil

2 dl red wine

**Stock/ sauce:**

5 dl stock (made of bones of wood grouse)

2 onions

3 carrots

1 dl cream

3 tablespoons wheat flour

Mix the ingredients for the marinade. Remove the legs, wings and breast pieces of the wood grouse and leave to marinate for four hours. Meanwhile let the bones boil. Lard the breast pieces and legs with American bacon. Put them to fry in an oven dish for a couple of hours at 180 centigrades. Make a sauce of the dripping and bone stock. Let simmer for about half an hour and season. Improve the taste with cream. You can thicken the sauce with wheat flour. Serve with carrot timbale.

# OCTOBER

It is the time for slaughtering. First the lamb was slaughtered and as it was still quite small it was eaten up soon. Next it was the pig's turn as it cannot bear the cold.

Then the calf born in spring was slaughtered and put into salt as a whole. The meat was brought to a barn – in this region we don't need freezers.

A lot of fishing has to be done before the first snow, covering the rivers, falls. It is easy to catch burbots in autumn and also vendance roe is best at this time of the year.

An extended family had to live on fish as long as possible and only few knew where to catch the biggest roaches. Sometimes even a whitefish could be caught.

ROAST RABBIT . . . . . . . . . . . . . . . . . . . . . 60

RABBIT TERRINE
WITH CURRANT SAUCE . . . . . . . . . . . . . . 60

FRIED PORK GRAVY . . . . . . . . . . . . . . . 60

SALTED VENDACE . . . . . . . . . . . . . . . . . . 62

MUTTON CABBAGE . . . . . . . . . . . . . . . . . . 62

TURNIP-WHEAT BREAD . . . . . . . . . . . . . . 62

WHIPPED LINGONBERRY PUDDING . . . . . . 62

CURRANT SAUCE . . . . . . . . . . . . . . . . . . 62

VENDACE ROE AS HORS-D'ŒVRE . . . . . . . 62

MUTTON CHOPS IN
GARLIC-HERB-CREAM . . . . . . . . . . . . . . 63

LINGONBERRY-CREAM PUDDING . . . . . . . 63

CARROT-OATCHIPS . . . . . . . . . . . . . . . . . . 63

## ROAST RABBIT

| |
|---|
| 2 rabbits |
| 1/2 kg greasy spare ribs or |
| 2 packets American bacon |
| 4 carrots |
| 4 onions |
| salt, lovage |

Cut the rabbits, spare ribs (bacon), carrots and onions into pieces and place them in a casserole dish, the pork on top. Cover scantily with water, season and let simmer in the casserole in low heat (150 centigrades) for at least four hours.

## RABBIT TERRINE WITH CURRANT SAUCE

| |
|---|
| *(4 servings)* |
| 400 g rabbit (leg meat) |
| 100 g pork |
| 1 chopped onion |
| 1/2 dl stock |
| 2 dl cream |
| 1 egg yolk |
| 2 tablespoons dried boletus |
| 2 teaspoons crushed juniper berries |

Mince the rabbit and pork in food processor. Add the cream, yolk, chopped boletus, stock and spices. Place the mixture in a greased oven-proof dish. Lower the heat and put the lid on as soon as the mixture gets some colour. Let simmer in the oven until tender.

## FRIED PORK GRAVY

| |
|---|
| *About 700 g lightly salted fatty pork* |
| 2 tablespoons wheat flour |
| 1 onion |
| 1 dl cream |

Rinse the meat, drain and cut into slices, keep turning in wheat flour and fry in hot fat. Stir in water and the chopped onion. Let simmer under the lid until the meat feels tender. Add the cream before serving.

*Marinated boletus, rabbit terrine, wood grouse roast, stuffed willow ptarmigan, carrot and beet timbale, rabbit roast, mushroom steaks, 'puikula' potatoes, game sauce and potherb sauce.*

## SALTED VENDACE

1 kg vendace

200 g salt

Clean the fish, but do not remove the heads. Place vendace and salt in layers in the dish and a small weight on top.

## MUTTON CABBAGE

1 kg shoulder and breast of mutton

1 white cabbage head

2 tablespoons salt

1 dl syrup

5 allspices and white peppers

thyme, chopped lovage

1/2 l water

Wash the meat and cut into small pieces. Put the big cabbage and meat chunks for a second on a frying pan. Place the meat chunks and cabbage as well spices in a casserole dish in layers and add the water. Let the stew simmer slowly under a lid for 2-3 hours. In the stew you can also serve potatoes peeled raw and cut into sli-ces. Stir them in the stew when meat and cabbage have simmered medium tender.

## TURNIP-WHEAT BREAD

3 dl milk or water

2 tablespoons yeast

salt, wheat flour

1 1/2 dl grated turnip

Take the grated turnip and mix in lukewarm liquid. Add the yeast and salt and make a rather thick dough. Knead plaits or round balls and bake them in 225 centigrades after they have risen.

## WHIPPED LINGONBERRY PUDDING

1/2 l lingonberries

2 l water

2 dl sugar

2 dl semolina

1-2 dl potato flour

Rinse the berries, crush and boil in water until no juice is left. Strain. Add the sugar to boiling lingonberry juice. Fold the semolina into the mixture. Let simmer for 20 minutes. If required thicken with potato flour mixed with water. Bring to a quick boil. Pour the pudding to a plate and sprinkle sugar on top. Serve cold. You can also beat the pudding until spongy. Then potato flour is not required.

## CURRANT SAUCE

4 dl blackcurrants

4 cl currant wine

1 dl sugar

(juice)

Boil the currants and sugar until the berries break. Mix in a blender and put through a strainer. Add the currant wine. If the sauce is too thick add some juice.

## VENDACE ROE AS HORS-D'ŒUVRE

8 slices dark bread

200 g vendace roe

2 onions

sour cream, chopped dill, black pepper

Cut the bread slices into rounds. Mix the roe with chopped onion. Pipe sour cream on the edges of the bread slices. Place the roe and chopped onion in the middle and sprinkle black pepper on top.

## MUTTON CHOPS IN GARLIC-HERB-CREAM

3 chops per diner

**Sauce:**

about 1 dl three kinds of herbs

e.g. rosemary, thyme and chervil

garlic

3 dl cream

2 dl stock

1 tablespoon butter

1 tablespoon wheat flour

Chop the herbs. Press garlic, roll in butter and add the wheat flour. Pound the chops under

wrap, fry in butter, pour the sauce over and let simmer a moment.

## LINGONBERRY-CREAM PUDDING

300 g curd

2 dl lingonberry juice

3 egg yolks

1 dl milk

100 g sugar

6 gelatines

1.5 dl cream

**Sauce:**

about 150 g lingonberries

1 dl sugar

a little water

Mash the ingredients of the sauce. Beat the yolks and sugar well. Add the milk brought to quick boil blending well the yolk mixture. Put on a stove and heat until it thickens. Do not boil! Press the water out of the gelatines and stir in the boiling mixture. Season with sugar. Chill,

add the curd and juice and at last the whipped cream. Place in serving dishes or a cake mould and let set.

## CARROT-OATCHIPS

3 dl sugar

1/2 dl syrup

1/2 dl cream

1.5 dl melted butter

2 dl oat flakes

2 dl wheat flour

1 teaspoon baking powder

1 dl grated carrots

Mix all the ingredients. Make small balls of the batter and place on a baking sheet not too near to each other. Bake until golden brown at 175 centigrades. Do not remove until a little cool and lift on top of the base of a coffee cup. Press the bottom smooth and remove when completely cold.

# NOVEMBER

I t is the month of mysticism - and the time to enjoy meals. First preparations for the Christmas season are made. The pre-Christmas period is the time for celebrations ,Christmas parties are organized, not only in the holiday centres. There is a wonderful smell of ham and grog, and music invites to dance.

As days are getting shorter candles are lit - it's the time to enjoy new recipes. Northern lights can be seen in the sky, a breathtaking experience for reindeer drivers and Japanese tourists alike.
November is also the month of reindeer. The smell of life and death is in the air when Lapps gather at the 'separation of reindeer' meeting.

BUTTERMILK LOAF . . . . . . . . . . . . . . . . . 67

RYE BREAD & RAW-SPICED
SALMON SALAD . . . . . . . . . . . . . . . . . . . 67

MASHED POTATO SOUP . . . . . . . . . . . . . . 67

CARROT-LINGONBERRY-COMPOTE . . . . . . 67

REINDEER MEAT-CHEESE-PIE . . . . . . . . . . . 68

STUFFED REINDEER FILLET . . . . . . . . . . . . 68

LIQUEUR-PANCAKES FRIED
ON THE BOTTOM OF FIREPLACE . . . . . . . . . 68

## BUTTERMILK LOAF

1 l buttermilk

2 dl syrup

100 g yeast

2 tablespoons crushed orange peels

750 g rye flour

1 tablespoon salt

1 tablespoon crushed fennel

Heat the buttermilk and stir in part of the rye flour and yeast dissolved in a little water. Let the dough rise. Boil the syrup and spices quickly and add to the risen dough when chilled. Knead the rest of the flour to the dough at the same time. When the dough has risen again bake 3-4 loaves. Prick after they have risen, brush with hot water and bake in good oven temperature until light and ripe. Brush the loaves again shortly before removing them from the oven.

*Yeast bread, oatmeal bread, buttermilk loaf, blood bread and brown bread are part of the Lappish dinner table.*

## RYE BREAD & RAW-SPICED SALMON SALAD

Cube lightly dried ryebread slices to the size of a sugar lump. Roast lightly on a frying pan. Cut the raw-spiced salmon into small cubes. Place the ryebread and salmon cubes in layers in a bowl. Sprinkle with a little french salad sauce. Let rest overnight. Pile the salad either on a plate or on a serving dish in layers with a crispy salad, cucumber and pepper. Garnish with egg pieces, dill, raw-spiced salmon and capers.

## MASHED POTATO SOUP

2 l water

5 potatoes

2 carrots

1 onion

salt

white pepper or paprika

Put the chopped onion, cut potatoes and grated carrots into cold water and let simmer until the potatoes mash. Season with salt and white pepper.

## CARROT-LINGONBERRY-COMPOTE

1 l lingonberries

4 dl grated carrots

3 dl sugar

1 teaspoon red melantine

Boil the lingonberries until they break. Add the sugar, grated carrots and gelatine mixed with a little water. Let simmer a couple of minutes and remove the scum from the surface. Tin the compote into clean tins and shut immediately.

## REINDEER MEAT-CHEESE-PIE

| |
|---|
| 3 dl wheat flour |
| 150 g butter |
| 1 egg |
| 3/4 dl oat brans |
| **Filling:** |
| 300 g leek |
| 200 g Lappish cheese |
| 100 g smoked reindeer |
| 2 1/2 dl cream |
| 1/2 teaspoon herbal salt |

Cut butter into pieces, add wheat flour and mix slightly. Add the eggs, mix well with the batter crumbles and finally stir in the oat brans. Spread the batter into a greased mould and keep cool while making the filling.

## STUFFED REINDEER FILLET

| |
|---|
| *(1 serving)* |
| 150 g reindeer tenderloin |
| 30 g raw-spiced or coldsmoked salmon |

Press a hole in the middle of the reindeer fillet and push a salmon slice inside. Season with salt and white pepper. Fry until brown. Thicken the dripping with cream and blackcurrant jelly. Serve with seasoned vegetables, vegetable loaf and fried potatoes.

## LIQUEUR-PANCAKES FRIED ON THE BOTTOM OF FIREPLACE

| |
|---|
| *(about 25 pieces)* |
| 2 l milk |
| 400 g wheat flour |
| 100 g barley flour |
| 3 eggs |
| 2 dl melted butter |
| pinch of sugar and salt |
| **Filling:** |
| 1 l cloudberries |
| cloudberry liqueur |
| **on top:** |
| 5 dl cream |
| 1/2 dl honey |

Make the filling the previous day by marinating the cloudberries in liqueur. Let rest in a cool place. Stir in the flour, spices and melted butter. Let thicken for two hours. Fold into the eggs beating strongly. Fry the lace like surfaced pancakes in butter. Place liqueur flavoured cloudberries on the pancake, wrap into roll and garnish with whipped cream and cloudberries seasoned with honey.

*Salted vendace (page 62),*
*mutton cabbage (page 62),*
*lamb chops and garlic-herb-cream (page 63)*

# DECEMBER

C hristmas is near. The delicious smell of
cooking and baking is in the air. Stars are
twinkling in the sky and candles are lit. It's the time to
look back, to thank, to give and receive presents.
Good food also belongs to the Christmas season. Ham,
game, salmon and trout are part of a traditional
Lappish Christmas meal. The special red Christmas
fish and also reindeer can be served on Christmas
Eve.

Although life used to be hard, there always were
plenty of things to eat at Christmas. We had meat,
pastries, creamed rice and plums. Just in
time our self-made candles appeared
on the table and also 'himmelis', those
traditional mobiles made from straw
and decorated with gingerbread were made.

COOKED LOAF . . . . . . . . . . . . . . . . . . . . . 72

RED RAW-SPICED SALMON . . . . . . . . . . . . . 72

LINGONBERRY
RAW-SPICED WHITEFISH . . . . . . . . . . . . . . 72

REINDEER CALF ASPIC . . . . . . . . . . . . . . . 72

REINDEER ROAST . . . . . . . . . . . . . . . . . . . 72

CHRISTMAS-RED
CHRISTMAS FISH . . . . . . . . . . . . . . . . . . . 73

HEAVENLY DISH . . . . . . . . . . . . . . . . . . . .74

SAUTEED REINDEER . . . . . . . . . . . . . . . . . .74

## cooked loaf

| |
|---|
| 6 dl water |
| 3 dl syrup |
| 100 g yeast |
| 1/2 tablespoon salt |
| 800 g rye flour |
| about 1 kg wheat flour |

Press the dough into a greased dish equipped with a lid. Let rise nearly double its size. Place the dish into boiling water for five hours. Be careful not to allow any water into the dish. Open the lid, tip and let cool. Eat with butter or cream cheese.

## red raw-spiced salmon

| |
|---|
| 350 g salmon |
| coarse salt |
| sugar |
| grated beet |

Sprinkle coarse salt on the bottom of a dish and put the salmon fillet on top. Sprinkle coarse salt on the fillet, a little sugar and the grated beet topmost. Eat the following day.

## lingonberry raw-spiced whitefish

| |
|---|
| 750 g whitefish fillets |
| coarse salt |
| 2 tablespoons sugar |
| 10 white peppercorns |
| 2 dl mashed lingonberries |

Place the whitefish fillets skin-side down on the chopping board. Sprinkle the coarse salt sugar mixture on top. Crush the whole white peppercorns and sprinkle on top. Spread the mashed lingonberries on greaseproof paper and place the fillets on top. Wrap a tight parcel and let rest overnight. Remove the mashed lingonberries. Serve with 'puikula' potatoes and rye bread.

## reindeer calf aspic

| |
|---|
| 1 kg bony calf meat |
| 1/2 kg reindeer roast |
| 1 tablespoon salt |
| black pepper, allspices |
| 2 onions |
| 2 tablespoons vinegar |
| 1 carrot |
| 7 gelatines |

Cover the rinsed meats with cold water. Remove the scum. Add the spices, onion and carrot. Remove the bones and cut the meat into cubes. Place the meats into a sauce pan and pour the sprained stock over. Heat further and season with vinegar. Then stir in the dissolved gelatines. Pour to moulds to set. Ready to be eaten the following day.

## reindeer roast

| |
|---|
| 4 onions |
| 6 carrots |
| 500 g potatoes |
| salt, a pinch of rose pepper, butter |

Cut the roast into 4 cm thick slices. Slice also the peeled vegetables. Place potato, onion, carrot and meat slices in layers in a foil. Sprinkle spices in between. Wrap the foil well. Let fry for

1.5 hours in low temperature in baking oven in an earthenware.

## CHRISTMAS-RED CHRISTMAS FISH

*750 g salmon or trout fillets*

**Stock:**

*3 dl beet juice*

*1/2 dl medium sweet white wine*

*2 tablespoons red wine vinegar*

*2 tablespoons oil*

*salt*

Cut thin slices of the fish fillets and place in a bowl. Pour over the stock and leave to marinate until the next day in a refrigerator. Can be preserved in the marinade for 4-5 days.

*In the first row a reindeer fillet stuffed with raw-spiced salmon, cloudberries, Lappish cheese, spruce shoot syrup, onion, whitefish roe, red raw-spiced salmon and heavenly dish. In the middle the marinated mushrooms, salted vendace, rabbit terrine, blueberry raw-spiced whitefish, reindeer meat-cheese-pie (page 68), reindeer calf aspic, reindeer roast, Christmas breads and a barley bread.*

## heavenly dish

Moisten thin slices of delicious coffee bread in a sugar-milk mixture. Pile layers of strong plum fool, coffee bread, boiled plums and whipped cream to a dish. Top this delicacy with cream and plums. Eat on Christmas evening.

## sauteed reindeer

Cut thin chips of a frozen reindeer roast. Have 1/4 kg meat per diner. Put the frozen chips to a cast iron pot where there is already melted butter, pork fat and reindeer fat. Let simmer about 15 minutes and add liquid if needed. If you use frozen sauteed reindeer, the cooking time is longer. Season with coarse salt. Sauteed reindeer can be seasoned additionally with onion, allspice or whipped cream. Serve with mashed potatoes, buttered potatoes or boiled potatoes. Serve with pickled cucumber and lingonberries.

*Christmas breakfast: Dried meat and raw-spiced salmon with barley bread, Christmas porridge.*

# hullu poro's courageous landlady

Being an entrepreneur requires two essentials - you should enjoy your work and have a strong belief in what you're doing. Listen to your soul and do not hesitate to obey your feelings as interhuman relations are of major importance when doing business - a fact even known by bankers. According to Päivikki Palosaari's motto of survival, a balanced relation between mind, matter and money is indispensable. Visions can only be realized as long as money is available and money is also of vital importance when developing new ideas. Nevertheless, first of all you have to have an idea says Lapland's courageous entrepreneur. That is Päivikki Palosaari's art of living.

As a child Päivikki had plenty of jobs. She started her career as a temporary worker, helping to harvest hay, to peel potatoes or onions. At the age of 15 she slaughtered a calf, worked at the construction site 'Vesisaari' and learned to fish with the long fishing line. She travelled on board of a sailing ship to Tunisia working in the ship's restaurant, and finally returned to Kittilä at the age of 24 starting work as a chef in the hotel Levitunturi.
Päivikki Palosaari loved her work, still, she dreamed of a business of her own. She started to run a small kiosk and soon after bought an old holiday resort in a village nearby. This was the start for her Hullu Poro project which is constantly growing – and Päivikki, reaching for the stars, just recently opened the Taivaanvalkeat, a new holiday centre. The entrepreneur Päivikki enjoys her work and loves to pass on her enthusiasm to visitors coming to her place.

How did the idea of 'Hullu Poro' arise? Päivikki is sure - her best and most daring ideas develop in her subconscious. The Hullu Poro story almost sounds like a saga when people from Levi pass it on. It's in a dream, far, far away at a hidden place somewhere on a fell. It's crisp cold. The moon is shining, spreading its blood-red light over the landscape. Twinkling stars and polar lights brighten the scene. A reindeer, its antlers all white, is slowly moving through a valley. Then the eery impression of a reindeer sledge appears among dwarf birches. The sledge swaying like a boat in a storm makes its way across snow-covered stems and stones. Päivikki half asleep, watches the surrounding, the slowly moving shadow of the reindeer sledge and the shadows of the trees. All of a sudden the sledge turns over and the reindeer hits its head against a tree stump. From behind the mountain voices appear - screams of harassed souls and howling wolves. Next it's quiet again. Päivikki rests, opens her rucksack, eats some of the dried reindeer gammon and falls asleep. Wind starts to blow and as it is getting stronger the sound of howling wolves can be heard again. The reindeer jumps up and starts to dance a devil's dance around the fire. Evil spirits appear in the form of a reindeer. It dances wildly and approaching the fire it tries to chase Päivikki away into the cold of the night. Päivikki without hesitating heads towards her rucksack, eats a whole fly agaric and takes a long swig from a brandy bottle. She starts to beat her drum furiously, goes into trance and starts uttering magic spells. Fighting heavily against the evil spirits she finally reaches distant realms. Again she utters ancient magic spells, also known to her ancestors. The charms act, the earth's crust breaks, the interior becomes visible and all she sees is joy, love and happiness. Giving off sparks, the evil spirits vanish leaving behind a funnily dancing reindeer - the 'hullu poro'. Päivikki rises and continues her travel watching

the northern lights. This is the spot where the restaurant Hullu Poro has been built, Levi's famous restaurant. And close to this place, in the small town Köngäs you can now also find the Taivaanvalkeat.

Päivikki Palosaari knows to estimate the preciosity of Lapland's nature not only for her work in the tourism branch. Nature and woods are god, religion and culture in one for Päivikki. Lapland's nature has a lot to offer. Tourists may be amazed by the mighty calmness of the beautiful fells, barren screes, the tremendous moorlands, green riversides and by the mild climate, influenced by the Gulf Stream. It's one of the earth's last paradises, says Päivikki.

The January sky in Köngäs is glowing red and northern lights can be seen at night. There is a steadily growing restlessness. Now, it's only a matter of days until the rising sun will act like an artist, painting the landscape in pastel colours and eliminating a clear border between earth and sky. February is the month of pure white snow. Rest on this soft and silky cushion and let your mind run free. What used to be black now turns into white. The horizon widens and the mind becomes clear. Single foggy patches cover the sun now and then and birch-

*This is one of the earth's last paradises, says Päivikki.*

es spread their branches as if they were welcoming spring. March and April play with the frisky mood of the springlike winter until the glistening snowfields disappear. It's a grey morning in spring. Birches are swaying in the wind waiting for the summer to come. May - this is the time when the earth comes into being again. A newborn reindeer calf, its legs still shaking, listens to the gently blowing wind on the fells. A new day begins and the smell of springtime is in the air. Snow is melting. Here and there first brown patches of earth can be seen, the sound of water rushing down the mountains is increasing as frozen rivers start to melt. The breaking ice reminds of crying cranes. It smells of earth. Finally it's June, leaves start to grow and the brown colour of the ground turns green. In a few weeks' time seasons are changing - it's summer. Around Midsummer's day plenty of globe flowers, dandelions and buttercups are in bloom turning the landscape yellow.

Lakes and rivers still cool down at night and rivers are veiled in mist. The sun shines night and day, and the peaceful calmness resting on rivers at night is only disturbed by the first morning breeze. July - it's the time of blue flowers and ripening blueberries. Cloudberries turn moorlands golden-yellowish in the end of the month. The heart-rending blossom of the willow herb dominates in August - a sign that 'ruska' is close. An overwhelming blaze of col-

ours covers Lapland in September. It's the time of ruska - Lapland's Indian summer. Soon autumn storms will shake the trees, blowing away thoughts as coloured leaves. In October time stops resting in blackness. Only the fells, whose words are carried away by wind, remain. What is time when you are directly confronted with moments. Everything rests waiting for the snow to come. The first snow flake is like a tear, the immutable perpetual change - it's winter. November is the month of survival. Its typical blue light revives creative powers and nature resembles a fairytale world.

Finally it's Christmas. It is the feast of the Lappish people and the whole country is covered with small lights. Bells are ringing, stars are twinkling in the sky and red cheeks spread their colour redding the morning northern lights. This is Päivikki's romantic view of a close relationship between man and nature in Lapland.

Päivikki Palosaari was born in Köngäs, a village belonging to the municipality Kittilä. Her father was a farmer, her mother midwife - and in a way Päivikki's work connects to her mother's job as she constantly hatches new ideas. When proceeding with new plans she knows she can trust her feelings, her instincts and her mind. Living in an arctic area, as for instance Lapland, implies that people have to

cope with hard conditions. Surviving in this sensitive natural surrounding is rather an art of living nowadays. Päivikki's strong willpower becomes obvious when looking at a teenager photo. Her leadership abilities developed early and all she was dreaming of was to own a hotel or a restaurant. In her early childhood she was wondering what the meaning of the word 'self-financing' would be... There's a twinkle in her eye as she tells the story of her former life - she believes she had been married to an Indian fabric trader! The tenacious character of the northern woman could already be seen at an early age. Her grandmother used to say she'd 'walk right through the hardest stone'. She inherited a creative spirit and a yearning for religious matters from her grandmother and her mother. Iris, her mother cultivates intuitive sensitivity, is interested in metempsychosis, Far Eastern religions and nature healing.

Doing business in the tourism branch requires a lot of energy, sensitivity, a certain feeling for business affairs and knowledge how to handle stress. It is essential never to disappoint clients. People naturally feel the need to recreate themselves and this has to be taken seriously. Holiday is therapy for the psyche and travellers should receive the best service. The shaman-culture also offers ways for the psyche to have a rest. Laplandís mysticism plays a major role at the Taivaanvalkeat. Travellers can enjoy a peaceful atmosphere, listen to their heartbeat and loosen up.

We were taught that everything has to be taken calmly. Positive thinking and impulsiveness had to be eradicated, our vivacity was suppressed. We had to be quiet in school, in the sauna, when eating supper - we had to be quiet just everywhere. Nevertheless, people are creative and the Taivaanvalkeat is the place where it is possible to find out how much of that creativity is waiting for inspiration. In the middle of this peaceful nature people have the chance to get lost in thoughts. It's time to relate to the expansiveness of the environment. In a temple in the yard or in the Lappish 'seita' people have the possibility to relate to spiritual powers.

Human beings are about to alienate from nature. Thus, it may happen that children living in big cities make drawings of fish sticks when asked to draw a fish. And only few children experience how to milk a cow or how to harvest potatoes. The Taivaanvalkeat offers the opportunity to learn traditional manual skills. Here it is possible to produce Lappish cheese, to cook at an open fire, to harvest berries and a lot more. Experience the traditional Lappish life style as it used to be some generations ago.

Päivikki's family always worked a lot. All of their food usually came from the surrounding nature. Whatever they had to eat depended on the season of the year. In winter they mostly had meat, and in summer cooked or grilled fish every day. Päivikki's father used to catch pikes, perches, roaches and trouts. Whenever a pike could be found in the net this was a reliable sign that bad weather was coming up! Lots of mushrooms had been eaten in autumn, and in winter naturally reindeer and game. Salad or vegetables – Lappish people called it 'hay' – had been regarded as unsuited for humans to eat. Whenever Lapps catch salmon it has to be eaten fresh – it will never end up in a freezer. This is also part of the tradition of Hullu Poro's kitchen. A further and very important principle is that all of the food prepared in Hullu Poro's kitchen has to come from Lapland. And there's also the wise and traditional principle to be economical. You may not to waste God's gifts. According to Päivikki the work of a good cook has to be hygienical, economical, quick, imaginative and creative.

The secrets of the kitchen of Hullu Poro are hidden in the basic foodstuff used. Reindeer meat, game, birds, berries, mushrooms, herbs, fish and vegetables. Savoury and deliciously looking food can only be prepared when using tasty and fresh ingredients. And according to the time of the year colours on the table are changing. Päivikki loves to create a pleasant milieu and a friendly service is of general importance to her. Excellent cooking is one of the main aspects in the tourism business. The pleasant smell of food should be like a warm hearted welcome to the visitors.

The microwave was still to come when Päivikki started her work in Lapland's kitchens. At that time salad consisted of a mixture of several vegetables. Peas, cauliflower, carrots and beans. The most superb dinner of the house was 'Reindeer Filet Maaret', consisting of reindeer filet, fried salmon and rice. The meal was topped with chanterelle cream and customers always enjoyed this special meal.

Then, in the 1980's Chinese cabbage found its way into Lappish kitchens. Päivikki learned to prepare vegetables such as kohlrabi, white cabbage, Brussel sprouts, broccoli and salad with all kinds of dressings in her childhood. Nevertheless, the situation has changed. Today, people grow herbs, vegetables and berries in greenhouses in all parts of Lapland. The direct marketing of the products is common today. All products are of high quality. They are clean and savoury and there is a remarkably wide range of products. Customers too are demanding. Tourists know what they are looking for and tour operators know where to search for corresponding offers. The inhabitants of Lapland are proud of their gastronomic culture and it's their interest to serve travellers coming from the south of Finland and from other parts of the world alike.

*Olli Tiuraniemi*

*The Taivaanvalkeat is Päivikki's lifework, the centre uniting mind and soul.*

# OWN
# RECIPES

# Seduced.

## Presidentti.

Made from
the world's best
grades of coffee.
From Paulig, naturally.

Paulig

hotelli
MERIHOVI
Keskuspuistokatu 6–8, FIN-94100 KEMI
Tel. +358-(0)16-458 0100
Fax +358-(0)16-458 0999

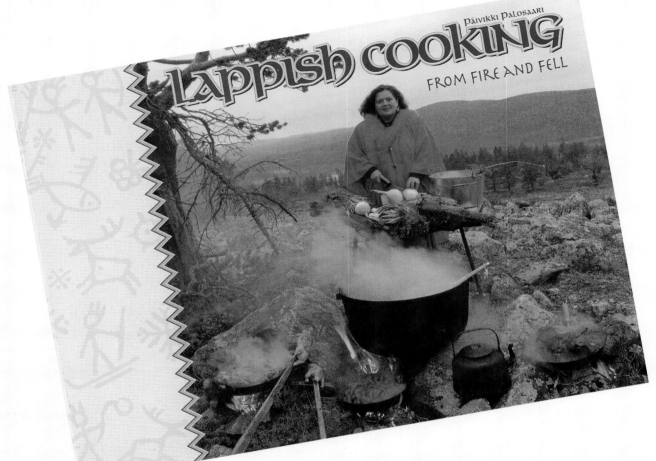

**Päivikki Palosaari**

# Lappish Cooking

## FROM FIRE AND FELL

*Tilaukset • Orders • Bestellungen*

Polarlehdet Oy, Katajaranta 24, FIN-96400 ROVANIEMI
Puh./Tel. +358 (0)16 311 611, Fax +358 (0)16 312 845
Internet: www.matkalehti.fi

KESPRO

www.kespro.com

**LEVI CENTER**
*hullu poro*

Levi Center Hullu Poro, 99130 SIRKKA
Telephone +358 16 651 0100
Fax +358 16 651 0260, +358 16 641 568 (Sales Groups)
E-mail: hullu.poro@levi.fi
Internet: www.hulluporo.fi

# Isännän parhaat viinit

Choix du Patron on viinisarja, jonka viinit edustavat laadukasta ja aitoa Ranskan maalaisaatelia. Ne ovat erinomaisia ruokaviinejä, jotka tuovat esiin eri ruokalajien parhaat puolet ja palkitsevat niin kokin kuin ruokavieraatkin.

Tässä esitellyt Choix du Patron -sarjan viinit tulevat Etelä-Ranskasta, Pyreneitten vuoriston ja Rhône-joen välissä sijaitsevalta hedelmälliseltä Languedoc-Roussillon-viinialueelta. Nämä viinit valmistetaan huolella ja rakkaudella rypäleistä, joiden alkukoti on ranskalaisessa maaperässä.

## Petit Coq

| | |
|---|---|
| *Rypäle* | *Cabernet Sauvignon* |
| *Väri* | *Tummanpunainen* |
| *Tuoksu* | *Melko runsas, viinillinen* |
| *Maku* | *Keskitäyteläinen, hyvärunkoinen, pehmeä* |

Pehmeä Petit Coq täydentää erinomaisesti perinteisten liharuokien sekä viinillä ja mausteilla höystetyn broilerin makua. Se on myös mainio juustojen seuralainen.

## Petit Vent

| | |
|---|---|
| *Rypäle* | *Sauvignon Blanc* |
| *Väri* | *Keltainen* |
| *Tuoksu* | *Raikas, herukanlehtimäinen* |
| *Maku* | *Kuiva, ryhdikäs, raikkaan hapokas* |

Sauvignon Blanc -rypäleistä valmistettu Petit Vent on kala- ja äyriäisruokien oiva kumppani. Raikkaan makunsa vuoksi se sopii myös seurusteluviiniksi.

## Petit Pont

| | |
|---|---|
| *Rypäle* | *Syrah* |
| *Väri* | *Syvänpunainen* |
| *Tuoksu* | *Puhdas, marjaisan hedelmäinen* |
| *Maku* | *Keskitäyteläinen, runsas, pyöreän tasapainoinen* |

Runsasvärisistä Syrah-rypäleistä valmistettu Petit Pont on erinomainen tumman lihan seuralainen, josta riittää makua lammasateriallekin. Petit Pont sopii erinomaisesti myös gratinoitujen kasvisruokien kanssa nautittavaksi.

## Petite Fleur

| | |
|---|---|
| *Rypäle* | *Chardonnay* |
| *Väri* | *Vaaleankeltainen* |
| *Tuoksu* | *Hedelmäinen, rehevän viinillinen* |
| *Maku* | *Kuiva, runsas, raikkaan tasapainoinen* |

Auringon kypsyttämille hedelmille tuoksuva Petite Fleur on parhaimmillaan kala- ja salaattiruokien kanssa nautittuna. Tämä moderni, runsasarominen viini on myös ihanteellinen aperitiivi ja seurustelujuoma.

Choix du
PATRON

Maahantuonti, pullotus ja markkinointi: Primalco Oy, puh. (09) 13305, www.primalco.fi
Tukkumyynti: Havistra Oy, puh. (09) 13304

STORAENSO™

*Uusi näkökulma.*

*Stora Enso Oyj*
*www.storaenso.com*

# A GOOD YEAR IN THE AIR.

Finnair has received many awards for its fine wine expertise. Our wine cellar in the air always offers the best: carefully selected red and white wines, the best of bubbly. The wine selection for our Business Class has been judged by connoisseurs to be the finest of any airline. Anywhere.

# SAARIOINEN
Puhtaasta luonnosta hyvää valmista ruokaa